ENHANCING
LEARNING ABILITIES

ENHANCING LEARNING ABILITIES

by

DR. CAROLYN SCOTT

Copyright © 2019 by Dr. Carolyn Scott

ENHANCING LEARNING ABILITIES

Increase Your Child's Possibilities at the Kitchen Table

All rights reserved. No part of this publication may be reproduced, distributed, or transmitted in any form by any means, including photocopying, recording, or other electronic or mechanical methods, without the prior written permission of the author. For permission requests, write to Dr. Carolyn Scott at cams138@aol.com.

Editor: Nadya DePontbriand

ISBN: 978-1-5457-4478-9

Library of Congress Control Number: 7571755881

First Printing: 2019

Manufactured and printed in the United States of America

Table of Contents

Table of Contents i
Dedication vii
Author's Motivation viii
Introduction x
What is a Learning Disability? 1
Why Use Games and Activities? 3
How to Use this Book 4
Section 1: Processing Speed 5
Processing Speed 6
Processing Speed: Activities 8
    Activity 1: Repeating Phrases 8
    Activity 2: Crossword Puzzles 9
    Activity 3: Handwriting 10
    Activity 4: Roving Colors 11
Processing Speed: Games 14
    Game 1: War Card Game 14
    Game 2: SET Card Game 16
    Game 3: Uno Card Game 17
    Game 4: Scrabble Board Game 18
    Game 5: Blink Card Game 19
Section 2: Memory 21

Memory 22
A. Short Term Memory 22
Short Term Memory: Activities 24
    Activity 1: Items on a Tray 24
    Activity 2: Repeating Phrases 25
    Activity 3: Picture Recall 26
    Activity 4: Visualization 27
    Activity 5: Mind Maps 28
    Activity 6: To Do List 31
Short and Long Term Memory: Games 33
    Game 1: Great States 33
    Game 2: Mind's I - Junior Edition 34
    Game 3: Concentration 35
    Game 4: STARE 36
B. Long Term Retrieval 38
Long Term Memory: Activities 40
    Activity 1: Mnemonic Cognitive Credit Cards 40
    Activity 2: Crossword Puzzles 43
    Activity 3: Handwriting 44
    Activity 4: Reviewing Information Learned 45
Section 3: Auditory Processing 46
Auditory Processing 47
Auditory Processing: Activities 48
    Activity 1: Discrimination of Word Pairs 48

Activity 2: Beginning/Ending Sound Discrimination 50

Activity 3: Phonemic Similarities 52

Activity 4: Identifying the Incorrect Word in a Sentence.. 54

Activity 5: Quick Draw - Lemonhead Monster 56

Activity 6: Lego Build 58

Auditory Processing: Games 59

Game 1: Listening Lotto 59

Game 2: Simon Says... 60

Game 3: BINGO 61

Game 4: Mad Gab... 62

Section 4: Visual Perception and Processing 64

Visual Perception and Processing........................... 65

Visual Perception and Processing: Activities.......... 67

Activity 1: Optical Illusions 67

Activity 2: Incomplete Pictures of Objects........... 70

Activity 3: Wordles... 72

Activity 4: Working with Word Problems............. 81

Activity 5: Spelling 82

Activity 6: Trampoline 83

Visual Perception and Processing: Games 84

Game 1: SET 84

Game 2: Monopoly.. 85

- Game 3: Battleship 86
- Game 4: Connect Four 87
- Game 5: Slamwich 88

Section 5: Logic 90
Logic 91
Logic: Activities 92
- Activity 1: Logical Thinking 92
- Activity 2: Word Play 96
- Activity 3: Survival 97
- Activity 4: Free Websites for Logical Thinking 99

Logic: Games 100
- Game 1: Backgammon 100
- Game 2: Gobblett or Gobblett Junior 101
- Game 3: Othello 102
- Game 4: Connect Four 103
- Game 5: Chocolate Fix 104

Section 6: Executive Functioning 106
Executive Functioning 107
Executive Functioning: Activities & Games 115
- Cursive Handwriting 115
- Monopoly Board Game 116
- Sorry Board Game 117

Glossary 118
Resources 120

Outside Programs 120
Academic: 120
PACE - Process and Cognitive Enhancement 120
FastForword 121
PhonoGraphix Reading Program 122
Outside Programs - Self Regulation 123
How Does Your Engine Run? 123
Why Try? 124
About The Author 125

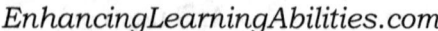

This page left intentionally blank.

Dedication

This book is dedicated to all students and their parents, who find the educational environment difficult, and to my three children who are always supporting me in my endeavors.

Thank you to Scotty and Melissa for always encouraging me to follow my dreams and to Odell, for making sure I did work on the book every day. I love each of you with all my heart.

Author's Motivation

The first question on everyone's mind when they know I am writing this book, is why? Well, hopefully this will explain my reason. My name is Carolyn Scott and I am a retired educator of 35 years. I spent my entire 35 years as a teacher and administrator in both traditional and non-traditional school settings. My experience includes working with students identified as having learning difficulties as well as emotional disorders. I was employed and retired from the School District of Hillsborough County, Florida where I worked with special education students in traditional middle schools and Juvenile Justice programs.

After retiring from the public-school system, I spent 15 years working in a charter school environment serving students with special needs.

My greatest passion is to help those students identified as having a learning disability and having parents understand what this means for their child in the school and home environment. Often, I have talked to parents about their child's difficulties in school; I discovered that they were not given a good understanding of how this affects the learning process. Often, after learning about their child's learning difficulty, the parents search for some avenue to help them. There are many good

EnhancingLearningAbilities.com

programs available outside of school to help those with learning disabilities, but they are expensive and take a strong commitment on the parents' part. With today's world, it often is out of the question for some families. If these programs are not an option for you, then this book is an attempt to help you assist your child be more productive in the learning environment. I will list several of the aforementioned programs in the Resource Section of this book in case you are interested in further research.

This book is an attempt to help parents give assistance to their students so that they can be successful in the part of life we call school, as well as help with future careers and life.

Please feel free to contact me at cams138@aol.com for questions or assistance.

Introduction

Whether you are having a family game night or working one-on-one with your child, you are already helping them to become a better learner. With this book of specific games and activities, you will be better equipped to work on the specific processing skills that are making it difficult for him or her to learn in school at the rate that is currently required.

These particular processing skills make it difficult to remember facts such as times tables and grammar rules (long term memory), forgetting to write down assignments, page numbers or important instructions (short-term memory), keeping up with lectures (processing speed) seeing the big picture (visual perception) or not being able to understand verbal lectures (auditory processing) because they often mistake words that are being said.

There are no "fixes" for a learning disability, but you can strengthen and learn strategies to work around these difficult areas. Learning disabilities are lifelong and children (and adults) need to learn both coping strategies and self-advocacy skills to use both in academic classes and in their life.

What is a Learning Disability?

Definition: A condition giving rise to difficulties in acquiring knowledge and skills to the level expected of those of the same age, especially when not associated with a physical handicap. (Note: There are many different definitions for a learning disability, and I could fill pages with them. However, I chose this definition as it shows the effect the disability can have in the academic environment).

Helping one's child who has a learning disability can be devastating to a parent. Especially, when the language used is not understandable to the typical parent. There are many programs that are useful for students who struggle to learn, but too many times they are too expensive or require skills that the parents do not have. It is so frustrating to see these children day in and out struggle to learn, and parents feel helpless to help them.

When a child has a learning disability there are certain processing skills that are not functioning correctly in the child's brain. These processes can manifest when trying to learn math, writing, or any other class that is required in school. It also can make simple directions and other academic tasks seem insurmountable to students identified as having a learning disability.

Some believe that tutoring will help these students be successful. It does help in the short term, but the underlying processes must be addressed if permanent changes are to be made.

Here is a list of the possible underlying processes that are weaker in students diagnosed as having a learning disability:

- Auditory Processing
- Long Term Memory
- Short Term Memory
- Visual Processing and Perception
- Processing Speed

Sections on Logic and Executive Functioning Skills Although these skills are not typical processing deficits, they will be included as they can be enhanced by using everyday materials on a regular basis and have a major impact on how a student does in school.

If you would like more information or would like to see how it feels to have a learning disability, I suggest that you watch the video by Rick Lavoie, The F.A.T. City Workshop, How Hard Can This Be? It is a wonderful video that lets you witness firsthand how it feels to have a learning disability and the behaviors that you can see when trying to navigate the school system.

Why Use Games and Activities?

Games and activities are a great way to learn. They make learning fun and motivating. It also leads to students following directions and engaging in team work. The outcomes of games-based learning are enhanced critical thinking skills, staying focused on one subject and being able to play and interact with others, which is critical in being successful in the learning environment and everyday life.

The activities and games are to be used in your day-to-day living. They can be used in the car, at the house, at the park, or anywhere you interact with your child. The games listed can be found at various stores but if you are looking for a bargain, you can always find them at yard sales. I have also listed "Additional Benefits" that can be gained by using the games and activities.

These games have been used with students, recommended and proved effective for students with learning disabilities by the following two organizations:
- ➢ **All Kinds of Minds**, originally owned and operated by Mel Levine, and now owned and operated by QED, Inc.
- ➢ **Pepin Academies of Hillsborough County** through their Skills Lab Instructor, Denise Morelli.

How to Use this Book

This book is divided into four parts that consist of the underlying skills that make learning difficult. Many of the games and activities will help in one or more areas. Sections 1 through 4 cover Processing Speed, Memory, Auditory Processing and Visual Processing. For example, if your child has difficulty in the area of processing speed only, just turn to Section 1: Processing Speed. If their weakness is in several sections, then use the games and activities in those appropriate sections. You will find some of the games and activities repeated in the various sections. Sections 5 and 6 include information on Logic and Executive Functioning Skills. Section 7 is the Glossary and Section 8 is a resource section.

For progress in your child, the games and activities should be completed at least three (3) times a week for 15 to 20 minutes. For maximum progress, games and activities should be played or completed at least 5 to 6 days a week for 15 to 30 minutes. Minimum results should be seen in 4 to 6 weeks if you follow the schedule. The longer you practice these skills, the more you will see progress.

Using all sections and playing the games and activities will never hurt your child. Strengthening areas of strength will also raise the bar on the deficit areas.

Enjoy and have fun!!!!

Section 1: Processing Speed

Processing Speed

Understood.org describes processing speed as a cognitive ability that can be defined as the time it takes a person to do a mental task. It is related to the speed in which a person can understand and react to the information they receive, whether it be visual, auditory or kinesthetic (movement).

Note: Any game or activity listed in this section or game you enjoy playing with your child can be used for increasing processing speed by setting a time limit and decreasing the time allowed when it becomes easy to complete the game or activity.

School Example: A teacher asks a question to the class and three questions later a student raises their hand and answers the first question that was given. It took that amount of time for the student to process each word of the question and determine what the question was asking.

My Personal Example: A teacher I worked with had a daughter that was attending a very prestigious private school. Although her daughter was very smart, it was hard for her to keep up with the work assigned. The private school has said if she could not keep up, she might have to transfer to a traditional school so she could utilize special accommodations. The school had set up a time for the daughter to be tested and if she was found to have a learning disability, she would most likely benefit from a transfer.

Upon learning of the SET game, my friend decided to give it a try. She played SET with her daughter every day and her daughter played the game by herself to practice. She became more and more proficient in increasing her processing speed. When testing time came, she was able to pass the processing speed portion of the test and was found not to have a learning disability. Her mother attributes her success to her using the SET game. Her daughter was able to stay at her private school, went on to college and today is a pre-school teacher!

Processing Speed: Activities

Activity 1: Repeating Phrases

While driving in the car or doing any type of chore, say a three-word sentence or three unrelated words and ask your child to repeat it right back to you. If they are successful with three words, increase to 4, 5, 6 words etc. until they can remember 10 words or a long sentence. You can make the words related (car, truck, van) or unrelated (car, pizza, Hawaii). The sentences can make sense or be made to be funny.

Additional Benefits: This activity also helps with increasing memory capacity.

Activity 2: Crossword Puzzles

Crossword puzzles are a great way to learn and come in a variety of types. They allow the child to see how much general knowledge of a subject or idea they know up front. Continued use of crossword puzzles will increase language skills. To begin, use an easy crossword puzzle or subject related puzzle. The best way to complete a crossword puzzle is to go down the "across" clues and fill in all the answers that you are sure are correct. Then complete the "down" clues that you are sure to be correct. This will give you letters in most words that will help you determine the correct word that fits in each slot. To help with processing speed, use a timer to set specific times for completion and then decrease the amount of time allowed.

Additional Benefits: With using crossword puzzles, you are also improving language and vocabulary, understanding directions (across vs down), understanding synonyms and antonyms and recall of general information from letters in filled-out words

Activity 3: Handwriting

This is an important skill that used to be taught in schools; however, there are a lot of students who were not given this instruction. You can still buy lined writing paper that is designed to help students visualize the size and practice of writing small and capital letters. This activity will require time given to it each day until the child is able to write in cursive on their own. To begin the cursive writing process, write the letters separately in cursive and then teach them how to connect the letters when used with various letters so that the flow is the most natural to make the word. To help with processing speed specifically, use a timer to set specific times for completion and then decrease the amount of time allowed.

Additional Benefits: Handwriting helps improve Executive Functioning skills such as planning and memory.

Resource: Cursive handwriting books are available at WalMart.com.

Activity 4: Roving Colors

For this activity, you will need 2-inch strips of construction paper in the colors of red, green, orange and blue. Cut strips into 2-or-3 inch squares. First, place the pieces in a row across the table leaving a gap between each square. Place one is always on the left, then place 2, place 3, then place 4 is on the right. To begin, place the squares in the following order:

Place 1 - Green
Place 2 - Orange
Place 3 - Red
Place 4 - Blue
Example:

    Place 1   Place 2   Place 3   Place 4

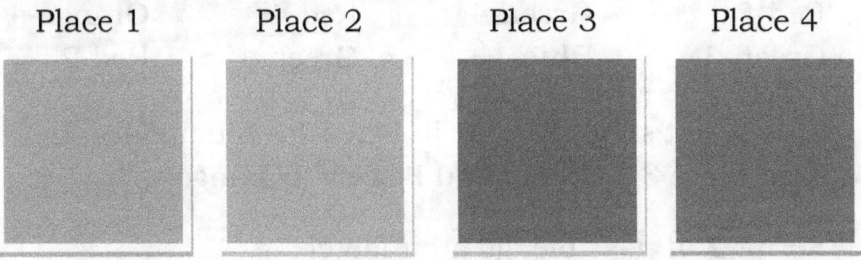

Give the child a color and a number and say, "I want you to move that one piece to the proper place". For example if I said: "Red 2", they would move the red piece to the second place; or if I say, "green four" the child would move the green square all the way to the fourth space.

For added auditory feedback have the participant repeat what the caller says. This is very beneficial with younger participants. To assist with processing speed, use a timer and see if they can improve the time it takes them to complete the game. Stress to the child that if they make an error, just keep going as it will come out fine in the end. Stress that it is about the skill building, not the outcome.

Script 1: Read starting with Column 1, Column 2, Column 3 and then Column 4.

Column 1	Column 2	Column 3	Column 4
Blue-2	Green-1	Orange-4	Orange-1
Blue-4	Blue-2	Green-4	Green-3
Orange-1	Red-1	Blue-4	Blue-1
Red-3	Green-4	Red-4	Orange-4
Green-3	Blue-1	Green-1	Red-2

This script should result in Place 1 – Blue; Place 2 – Red; Place 3 – Green; and Place 4 - Orange.

Script 2: If possible, go a bit faster

Column 1	Column 2	Column 3	Column 4
Orange-2	Orange-4	Red-3	Blue-1
Blue-4	Blue-4	Green-3	Orange-3
Green-4	Orange-4	Blue-4	Red-3
Red-1	Red-4	Red-2	Blue-4
Green-3	Blue-1	Orange-1	Orange-2

If directions are followed correctly, the outcome should be: Place 1 – Green; Place 2 – Orange; Place 3 – Red; and Place 4 – Blue.

You can also make up your own script if you would like.

Additional Benefits: Playing this activity will improve auditory processing (as they need to listen to the words in the directions), following directions and moving the construction squares to the right place.

Note: This activity was developed by Denise Morelli, Skills Lab Instructor at Pepin Academies - Riverview, FL.

Processing Speed: Games

Game 1: War Card Game

This game can be helpful in increasing processing time and being able to distinguish between lower and higher numbers. You can play with 2 to 4 players. If more than two players are playing, use two decks of cards.

Deal all cards out to each player face down (all should have equal cards). Each player will turn over the top card of their stack and the player with the highest value card wins. The winner takes the other players losing cards and adds them to the bottom of their stack. Play continues until players have cards of equal value facing up at which point "war" is declared. The cards from all players are placed in the center of the table, and each player makes a stack of three cards placed face down and a fourth card faced up. The player whose face-up card has the highest value wins all the cards in the center and his opponents' war pack. If the cards faced up are once again of equal value there is another "war" until a winner is determined. Regular play is then resumed and continues until one player wins all his opponents' cards.

Note: In the beginning, only play for 5 or 10 minutes at a time. The game can take up to 2 or 3 hours so start slow and make sure you note the time.

The overall objective is to see how long it takes him/her to identify the card with the largest value. It is better to start with only two players and add players as they become faster at selecting the highest card. When you are first playing, play near a clock with a secondhand and silently note the time it takes your child to determine the value. Each time you play, note the amount of time it takes. You should begin to see a difference in the time it takes them to select the highest card.

Additional Benefits: By playing this game you can also increase your math skills by:

> **Less, More Than:** When players throw down their cards, have the child with math difficulties say which card is higher in worth (or lower in worth).
>
> **Adding, subtracting and multiplying:** If your child is having difficulty with any of these three basic skills, have them add, subtract or multiple the value of the cards. This is easier if only two players are playing at one time.

Resource: Playing cards are available at WalMart.com and Amazon.com.

Game 2: SET Card Game

This card game was developed by the MENSA Society and gives practice for a variety of skills and requires you to match patterns (shape, number, design and color). The patterns must be either all the same in each of the 3 cards or each card must be different. Example: all 3 cards must be green or 1 card red, 1 card purple and 1 card green. See directions in card set for variations of game. For younger children, use only solid colors in the beginning.

Additional Benefits: SET is one of the most versatile games for children with a learning disability. It helps them be able to scan (which is needed in reading), recognizing patterns and sets (which is important in reading), visual processing (seeing the whole set of cards rather than each individual one separately and visual perception (recognizing the different colors, shapes, fillers and number of objects on a card).

Resource: This game can be found in most bookstores, on-line ordering sites and at setgame.com. The website also includes a free puzzle each day to solve. The puzzle requires you to find six sets of cards. The first three are pretty easy to find, but it gets harder as you find more sets.

This is a great family game, especially if you like competition!

Game 3: Uno Card Game

Deal each player 7 Uno cards face down. The rest of the cards are placed face down in a discard pile. The top card on the discard pile is turned over and the first player takes a turn. They must match the shown card on the discard pile by either number or color. For example, if the first card is a green 4, the first player may either put down a green card or a 4 card. If they have neither, they can play one of the wild cards if they have it in their hand.

Examples of wild cards are: Wild (you can change the color of the suit), Wild 4 (the next player in line must pick up 4 cards), skip (the next player is skipped), reverse (the direction moves back to the other side) or draw 2 (the player must draw 2 cards). When a player has only one card left in their hand, the player must yell out "Uno". The winner is the first player to not have any cards left to play.

Additional Benefits: The Uno game also helps with visual processing (seeing and recognizing the colors immediately), memory (what has been played earlier), and understanding and following directions.

Resource: Uno cards are available at WalMart.com.

Game 4: Scrabble Board Game

All tiles are placed face down on a surface. Each player selects 7 letter tiles from the surface and must make a word out of the letters and place on the playing board. Each player will then play off of the words the other player(s) created on their turn. You add up the points for the word each time a player plays a word. After each turn, you collect new tiles for the number of tiles you played on the board. The goal is to have the most points at the end of the game.

This game is a great family game that allows children to learn about competition and good sportsmanship. You can also play in pairs to begin with if language is limited.

Additional Benefits: Scrabble is a game that will help your child learn new language and increase spelling skills. It also helps with memory, as when they learn a new word, they are often able to recall it and use it in future games.

Resource: Scrabble is produced by Hasbro and is available at Amazon.com and Target.com.

Game 5: Blink Card Game

This card game is meant to be very fast-paced and anyone can play. It is better to have only two players in the beginning. Speed, observation, quick thinking and reflexes determine how the game will end.

To play the game (with 2 players) deal two equal draw piles of cards, giving one to each player. The cards at this time should not be seen by the player. Each player will take the top card from their pile and turn it face down between players. Then, each player draws three cards from the top of their pile which forms a "hand". At this time, the cards are turned over and players try to play cards from their hand on either of the two piles in the middle. For a card to be played, it must match at least one of the characteristics in color, shape or number of symbols on the card being played. For example, a card with 4 brown stars can be played on any card with brown (color), or has stars (shape) or a card with four symbols on it (number). Players must always have up to three cards in their hand at a time and draw from their own draw pile. Play continues until one player has played all their cards from their hand and their draw pile. Players can only play one card at a time.

Note: If neither player can match the top cards on either of the piles, play is paused, and players can draw the top card from their pile (if they still have a pile). If they do not have a pile, the player can pick one card from their hand and place it face up on the center pile. Play resumes as before.

Additional Benefits: With the fast pace of the game, Blink gives a release of energy to the player. It also assists with hand-eye coordination as they need to recognize and move at the same time in order to win the game.

Resource: Blink is produced by Mattel and is available at Amazon.com and WalMart.com.

Section 2: Memory

Memory

A. Short Term Memory

Short term memory is described on MedicineNet.com as a system for temporarily storing and managing information to carry out required complex cognitive tasks such as learning, reasoning and comprehension.

School Example: The teacher gives students the page number they need to turn to in the book and doesn't write it down on the board or overhead. The student is not able to hold the information into short term memory long enough to accurately complete the task and must ask again, and maybe several times, before they are able to get to the right place.

My Personal Example: This is an everyday occurrence for an older person, but it is certainly exasperating for someone young! This is true especially when a parent gives a chore for the child to do and they cannot remember it....the parent thinks the child is being obstinate and the child really can't remember all that was said.

I can certainly attest to this as a friend and mentor. I had a friend who had a son with ADHD (this was not a thing that long ago), which can impact short term memory, but unfortunately at that time did not understand what was happening. His parent would give him two or three chores to do around the house. He either completed the first or the last task but could not remember all of them. She thought he just didn't want to do them and would make up excuses. Imagine how she felt when I finally learned about short and long-term memory later and shared it with her. I felt bad for her as a mother that she did not understand what was really happening. It certainly was bad for both her son and herself!

Short Term Memory: Activities

Activity 1: Items on a Tray

This activity will require you to place three or four objects on a plate or tray and show it to your child for 15 seconds. Remove the plate/tray immediately and see how many of the items your child can remember. Make sure the items are not related in this activity. Example: paper clip, spoon, shampoo, clock. You will continue to add items to the plate/tray until you have reached about 15 to 20 items and they are able to recall them correctly. This requires the child to use a variety of memory strategies to remember all the objects such as categorization, visualizing, and using mnemonics.

Additional Benefits: Completing this activity will increase your child's ability to recall information, recognizing patterns (very helpful in reading) and recognizing sets.

Activity 2: Repeating Phrases

While driving in the car or doing any type of chore, say a three-word sentence or three unrelated words and ask your child to repeat it right back to you. If they are successful with three words, increase to 4, 5, 6 etc. until they can remember 10 words or a long sentence. You can make the words related (car, truck, van) or unrelated (car, pizza, Hawaii). The sentences can make sense or be made up to be funny.

You can use words from what your child is studying in school, which can help them with daily assignments. Example: Math vocabulary: exponents, multiplication, addition (then add other words one at a time)…product, quotient into, differences, etc.

Additional Benefits: Using new words that they are not familiar with helps improve and increase their language skills. For example, instead of using the word large, use a synonym like vast, huge, gigantic or immense.

Activity 3: Picture Recall

Find any picture in a magazine or paper and have the child study it for 2 minutes. Then remove the picture and ask them to give details as to what was in the scene. To begin with, they will remember only a few details, but as they practice more and more they should be able to recall details that are both shown and not shown. For example, if it is a beach scene then they can assume it is a nice sunny warm day. You can begin to ask more detailed questions as they become more proficient in recalling details.

Additional Benefits: This activity improves the skill of scanning, which is critical to reading and looking at information in textbooks. It also helps with noticing more details about a particular subject or information.

Activity 4: Visualization

Give your child a noun (dog, cat, fish, desk, table, etc) and ask them to close their eyes and visualize the item. Then ask them to describe the item in detail. At first, they may give one detail such as a large dog. Ask them questions one at a time and have them close their eyes again and see the item in more detail: What color? How many? What are they doing? Long hair or short hair? What kind are they?

Example: dog (noun) large or small, one color or more than one color, type of hair—long or short, where are they? (On a road, in the woods, in a yard.) What are they doing? (Running, walking, chasing something.)

The more detail they give back to you, the more they will remember. When they are studying school material, ask them questions that include details, so they can remember the idea, situation or effects better. Being able to visualize anything they are trying to remember will help them with details.

Additional Benefits: Visualization can be used in any subject or task given in school. It helps with remembering details, writing more descriptive sentences and increasing vocabulary.

Activity 5: Mind Maps

This activity can go along with visualization in that being able to draw a representation of what you are trying to learn will most likely give you more detail than just asking questions. This must be done at home, as it is likely not allowed in the school setting. Very few schools allow a student to show what they know by drawing, but when studying, it helps the child to remember facts and details more vividly.

After reading a passage and discussing a topic your child is studying at school, ask them to draw what they remember. Tell them to include as many details as possible in the drawing. As they begin this process, they might be able to recall only one detail or fact. They can continue to add to the picture as you study further on the subject.

See more information about Mind Maps on the next page.

Mind Maps by Tony Buzan

Mind Maps were originated in the 1960's and are used by millions of people when they want to use their minds in a different way. You can see examples of Mind Maps at tonybuzan.com.

What do you need to make a Mind Map?
- Blank unlined paper
- Colored pens and pencils
- Your Brain and…….
- Your Imagination!

7 Steps to Making a Mind Map

Step 1: Start in the center of a blank page turned sideways.

Why? Because starting in the center gives your brain freedom to spread out in all directions and to express it more freely and naturally.

Step 2: Use an image or picture for your central idea.

Why? Because an image is worth a thousand words and helps you use your imagination. A central image is more interesting, keeps you focused, helps you concentrate, and gives your Brain more of buzz!

Step 3: Use colors throughout.

Why? Because colors are as exciting to your brain as are images. Color adds extra vibrancy and life to your

Mind Map, add tremendous energy to your creative thinking, and is fun!

Step 4: Connect your main branches to the central image and connect your second and third-level branches to the first and second levels, etc.

Why? Because your brain works by association. It likes to link two (or three, or four) things together. If you connect the branches, you will understand and remember a lot more easily.

Step 5: Make your branches curved rather than straight-lined.

Why? Because having nothing but straight lines are boring to your brain.

Step 6: Use one key word per line.

Why? Because single key words give your Mind Map more power and flexibility.

Step 7: Use images throughout.

Why? Because each image, like the central image, is also worth a 1,000 words. So, if you have only 10 images in your Mind Map, it's already the equal of 10,000 words of notes.

Activity 6: To Do List

Do you ever give your child several items to complete and they either complete the first or the last one but not all? That is because they cannot keep the information in their head for that long and either remember the first or last item. To help with this, children who have short term memory deficits can utilize a to-do list that gives each step needed to complete the action or chore. If it is a young child, you can use pictures instead of words. For example, if the child has difficulty with remembering all the things to complete before leaving for school make a list of everything you want them to accomplish. They will have to check off each item as it is completed. That way, right before you leave you can visually see whether all items have been completed.

Samples of some To Do Lists are given on the following page. Feel free to copy or make your own depending on the needs of your family.

Additional Benefits: Learning to create To Do Lists will help your child with organization. Hopefully, they will also see how these checklists can help them with other subjects in school.

Checklists:

Examples of Checklists (for a child who cannot yet read, use pictures along with words)

Morning before School:
- Make your bed
- Brush your teeth
- Wash your face
- Get dressed
- Eat breakfast
- Grab school work

Before going to Bed:
- Brush your teeth
- Gather up homework and school work and put in organizers
- Put backpack or school materials by the front door
- Hang up your clothes
- Pick up your room

Short and Long Term Memory: Games

Note: The games listed can be used for both short-term and long-term memory.

Game 1: Great States

Great States is a state trivia game that uses a timer. It helps with memory as your child learns the location of all the states and their capitals. It is based on real life information as it requires you to buy exports, common industries and products in the states and move them around the country. This game can be played with the whole family. The player with the most money at the end wins.

Note: Each version of the game may have different rules and instructions.

Additional Benefits: Since geography is a major subject in the middle school grades, this game will help them identify where states, continents and countries are located. Additionally, it will assist with correct pronunciation of states and capitals.

Resource: Great States is produced by International Playthings and can be found at multiple stores including WalMart.com, Target.com and Amazon.com.

Game 2: Mind's I - Junior Edition

This game includes rolling a die to move tokens around a series of 6 different pyramids. Each pyramid has a specific category in which to answer questions. The pyramid categories are:

- Showbiz - charades
- Word Play - word knowledge
- Shape Shifter - patterns completion
- Learn by Heart - memorization
- Eye Spy - analogies and comparisons
- Pattern Play - pattern recognition

The first player (or team) to answer two questions from each category (pyramid) correctly must return to the center of the board and answer a final question to win the game. The game contains 450 questions and answer cards. You can use an egg timer to set time limits after the players have become more proficient in the game. This will help with processing speed.

Additional Benefits: This game will help your child increase their language abilities by understanding the different categories. They will also have practice recognizing patterns and learn the art of teamwork (if the game is played in teams), and when using a timer, increase processing speed.

Resource: Mind's I is produced by International Playthings and can be found at most stores including Amazon.com, WalMart.com and Target.com.

Game 3: Concentration

This game helps with visual memory and long-term retrieval of information. It is best to have the same age group of children play at one time. It is also better to have only two players at a time.

A pack of cards are shuffled well and dealt face down on a table so that no two cards touch. Cards should not be placed to allow for orderly rows and files. Each player, when it is their turn, turns two cards face up, one at a time, without moving either card away from its position in the layout. If the two cards are a pair, he/she removes them to his pile of pairs he has won and turns up two more cards. When he turns up two cards that are not a pair, he turns the cards face down, and the turn passes to the next player. The winner is the one with the most pairs after all cards have been turned over and collected as a set.

Additional Benefits: This game provides additional practice in being able to recognize patterns

Resource: Concentration can be found at WalMart.com, Target.com and Amazon.com.

Game 4: STARE

In this game, you draw a card and stare at the image, picture or scene for 20 seconds. Then you turn down the card and your opponent will ask you questions about the items you just saw on the card. As long as you continue to get the answers right, you keep going. When you miss a question, it is the other player's turn. Keep score. The player who answers the most questions correctly wins. Each question is worth one point.

Additional Benefits: This game or activity will increase your child's scanning ability, as well as being able to recall detail.

Resource: STARE is produced by Game Development Group and can be found at Amazon.com and Target.com.

Note: If you would rather not buy the game, you can use any picture, puzzle, scene from a TV movie, magazine, book etc. (as long as you can remember the details too!).

Special Note: There are many ways to help your child with short-term memory. Additional activities might include sub-vocalization, paraphrasing, summarization, diagrams, anagrams, rhymes and acronyms. These will be explained in the Glossary section of the book. (I really had to pick and choose which games and activities to include as there are so many ways to assist in this area.) After reading the definitions in the glossary and you want to expand the games and activities, please feel free to make up your own, or if you need assistance, please contact me.

B. Long Term Retrieval

Mel Levine, in his book, <u>Educational Care</u>, describes long-term memory as the ability to store the facts, ideas, and skills one needs to remember for a very long time.

School Example: These skills are required in learning multiplication tables, letter formation and critical personal data such as remembering your address and telephone number.

Personal Example: A middle school student was brought to me because he was unable to remember his multiplication facts. His mother had tried many ways to help him remember them with little success. I asked her if she allowed him to move around while practicing the tables. She said "No, I usually make him sit and I show him the problem and he had to give me the answer." During my time with him, I found out his favorite colors and used these colors to write the multiplication problems on cue cards. The harder sets (8's 9's, etc.) for him, we used his most favorite colors. Then, I allowed him to walk around the room while reciting and looking at the colored cards. After he rehearsed the times tables, I would have him walk around while I called out the multiplication tables to him and ask him to visualize it in his head (remembering the colors) before he answered. Within just a few weeks, he was able to memorize his multiplication tables with greater accuracy.

Long Term Memory: Activities

Activity 1: Mnemonic Cognitive Credit Cards

Cognitive credit cards are used so that students can check off each step needed to complete problems in math, complete writing steps or remember lists of items or mnemonics as necessary for the subject.

Students or parents can make these cognitive credit cards out of regular paper, construction paper in small sizes so that they fit in books, supply holders or notebooks that are required in the student's classes. You can color code them according to subject (social studies has a blue book, so use a blue cognitive credit card), etc.

Additional Benefits: Using cognitive credit cards gets the child used to listing items in a sequential manner and using acronyms to make and remember sentences and words.

Example: To remember the order of operations in math (PEMDAS), memorize the sentence, Please Excuse My Dear Aunt Sally.

P stands for parentheses, E is for exponents, M is for multiplication, D is for division, A is for Addition and S is for subtraction.

Cognitive Credit Cards – Mnemonics

HOMES – Geography
5 Great Lakes

H – Huron
O – Ontario
M – Michigan
E – Erie
S – Superior

PEMDAS – Math
Please Excuse My Dear Aunt Sally
P – Parenthesis (step 1)
E – Exponents (step 2)
M – Multiplication (step 3)
D – Division (step 4)
A – Addition (step 5)
S – Subtraction (step 6)

Rainbow Colors – Art
ROY G BIV

R – Red
O - Orange
Y – Yellow
G – Green
B – Blue
I – Indigo
V – Violet

FACT - Self Monitoring

F – Focus attention
A – Ask questions
C – Connect ideas
T – Try to picture important details

SQ3R - Reading

S – Survey
Q – Question
R – Read
R – Recite
R – Review

Planets - Science

My very eager mother just
served us nine pickles.

M – Mercury

V – Venus

E – Earth

M – Mars

J – Jupiter

S – Saturn

U – Uranus

N – Neptune

P – Pluto

Activity 2: Crossword Puzzles

Crossword puzzles are a great way to learn and come in a variety of types. They allow the child to see how much general knowledge of a subject or idea they know up front. Continued use of crossword puzzles will increase language skills. To begin, use an easy crossword puzzle or subject related puzzle. The best way to complete a crossword puzzle is to complete the "across" clues and fill in all the answers that you are sure are correct. Then complete the "down" clues that you are sure to be correct. This will give you letters in most words that will help you determine the correct word that fits in each slot. To help with processing speed, use a timer to set specific times for completion and then decrease the amount of time allowed. There are several sites on the internet that allow you to give them the words and they will develop a crossword puzzle for you.

Additional Benefits: By using crossword puzzles you are also improving language and vocabulary, understanding directions (across vs down), understanding synonyms and antonyms and exercising recall of general information from letters in filled-out words.

Activity 3: Handwriting

This activity is the hardest activity on children in school due to the amount of memory it takes to remember all the necessary steps in cursive writing. This is an important skill that used to be taught in schools; however, there are a lot of students who were not given this instruction and, I believe, shows why the deficit area of executive functioning skills has increased. You can still buy lined writing paper that is designed to help students visualize the size and practice writing small and capital letters. This activity will require time given to it each day until the child is able to write in cursive on their own. Begin with writing the letters separately in cursive and then teach them how to connect the letters.

Additional Benefits: Handwriting will increase the use of executive functioning skills such as planning, initiation and self-monitoring.

Resource: Cursive handwriting books can be located at WalMart.com.

Activity 4: Reviewing Information Learned

The best time to review information that is needed the next day is right before the student goes to bed and again in the morning for 5 to 10 minutes. This activity will help the student pull from memory the facts and details they need to remember for a quiz, test, or discussion.

Additional Benefits: This activity will increase recall of information, being able to orally give information and have a positive impact on using summarization skills.

Special Note: There are many ways to help your child with long-term retrieval. Additional activities that might be used includes: elaboration, paired association, open-ended questions, diagrams and activities that include visual, auditory and kinesthetic movement. These will be explained in the Glossary section of the book. After reading the definitions in the glossary and you want to expand the games and activities, please feel free to make up your own, or if you need assistance, please contact me.

Section 3: Auditory Processing

Auditory Processing

According to Understood.org, auditory processing disability is an inability to accurately process and interpret sound information (difficulty with recognizing subtle differences between sounds in words). An auditory processing learning disability is difficulty in analyzing and making sense of information that is taken in through the ears. This does not mean that there is difficulty "hearing" what you are saying, rather it affects how the information is interpreted or processed by the brain.

School Example: When the teacher is speaking about the weather the student hears hop instead of hot, which confuses the information the teacher is trying to explain.

Personal Example: This example is from my own experience. I honestly cannot remember how I learned to read, but I know it was not through phonics as I was in my 40's and doing a training through PACE (Processing and Cognitive Enhancement) that I realized that I could not hear the difference in vowel sounds when given to me individually. I had to remember the example of the word that gives the sound I was listening to before I could recite them. (Talk about embarrassing!!!!).
Example - Sound of vowels:
A - apple; E - egg, I - igloo, O - octopus and U - umbrella

Auditory Processing: Activities

Activity 1: Discrimination of Word Pairs

For this activity, you will verbally say two words and have the player determine if they are the same or different sounds. Example 1: pin - been. They are different sounds. Example 2: fox - fox. They are the same sounds. For your convenience, you will find examples of word pairs on the next page or you can make up your own pairs of words.

Additional Benefits: In this activity, you will come across homonyms or homophones that sound exactly alike, but have different spellings and meanings (their, there, they're). These types of words tend to confuse children especially when it comes to meaning and spelling.

Discrimination of Word Pairs: (d = different) (s = same)

hat – hat (s)
day – play (d)
cow – cowl (d)
rack – rack (s)
set – sit (d)
know – no (s)
clock – clack (d)
gate – gate (s)
not – knot (s)
read – read (s)
tale – tail (s)
sing – sigh (d)
blew – blow (d)
sty – sky (d)
sun – soon (d)
boom – boom (s)
rode – road (s)
bill – bale (d)

rack – rack (s)
rope – wrote (d)
set – sit (d)
beat – meat (d)
met – meat (d)
bob – bob (s)
neat – neat (s)
bean – been (d)
day – date (d)
pin – pine (d)
floor – floor (s)
raise – rise (d)
mate – mate (s)
pan – put (d)
eye – I (s)
blue – blew (s)
rode – ride (d)
there – their (s)

Activity 2: Beginning/Ending Sound Discrimination

For this activity, you will ask the child if words start and/or end with a specific sound that you give them.

Example 1: Do any of these words start with the sound "t": tennis, shoe, flight, tomatoes, tire?

Example 2: Do any of these words end with the sound "s": ice, is, miss, next, cup, lass.

You can make up your own words or you may use the samples on the next page.

Additional Benefits: This type of activity can also help with increasing language skills and recall of words.

Beginning and Ending Sounds: (y = yes; n = no)

Do these words start with the K (k) sound?

    corn (y)   ketchup (y)   cook (y)

    key (y)   car (n)   knock (n)

    truck (n)   bacon (n)   desk (n)

Do these words start with the L (l) sound?

    line (y)   fat (n)   lily (y)

    bike (n)   whale (n)   light (y)

    watch (n)   lady (y)   log (y)

Do these words start with the Ch "ch" sound?

    chop (y)   chestnut (y)   char (y)

    shadow (n)   certainly (n)   ship (n)

    slippery (n)   challenge (y)   cherish (y)

Do these words end with the N (n) sound?

    nine (y)   bench (n)   sun (y)

    long (n)   hen (y)   crane (y)

    numb (n)   nose (n)   skin (y)

Do these words end with the F (f) sound?

    have (n)   roof (y)   hit (n)

    if (y)   vase (n)   cough (y)

    life (y)   chef (y)   wash (n)

Activity 3: Phonemic Similarities

This activity requires the participant to tell what the phonemic similarities are between two words. Example: arm, ram (they both end in "m" sound); pillow - Sally (they both have the l sound in the middle of the word). You can use made up words yourself or you can begin by using the examples on the next page.

Additional Benefits: This activity will also assist with short-term memory as you need to remember the two words if given orally.

Phonemic Similarities

    bookcase – bear (b)   night – never (n)

    not – never (n)   dirt – sat (t)

    dogs – bees (s)   fur – door (r)

    pet – bell (e)   owl – ball (l)

    hat – hog (h)   dock – day (d)

    fir – firm (i)   moon – soon (oo)

    etch – reach (ch)   shadow – hello (o)

    cowboy – corn (c)   shower – away (w)

    zoo – zebra (z)   happy – supper (p)

    oranges – dungeon (j)   clock – clack (cl)

    gruff – great (gr)   fly – flip (fl)

    attend – baton (t)   ring – sing (ing)

Activity 4: Identifying the Incorrect Word in a Sentence

This activity requires the child to identify the incorrect word in a sentence when it is read aloud to them. Example: I *rally* don't know the answer. You can make up the sentences yourself or you can begin by using the examples on the next page.

This activity can be difficult at first as many of the words that are wrong are similar to the correct word. Start slow, but read the sentences at a normal rate.

Additional Benefits: This activity will help increase listening ability as well as memory as they will have to remember the words you have stated (short-term memory).

Identifying Incorrect Word in a Sentence

1. I *witch* I could go with you.

2. What do you *fink* about that?

3. Turn up the *rodeo* so I can hear that song.

4. The man used the *batter* to climb up the roof.

5. The *ramp* pole was lit well enough for us to see.

6. The large pig is *berry* fat.

7. Has the ice *green* been served yet?

8. Saturday means it is time to cut the *glass*.

9. Did you ever jump *hope* in elementary school?

10. The *garage* is the place to put trash.

11. Have you ever seen Big Ben - the *tock* in Europe?

12. Have the bananas gone *bed*?

13. The fireman put out the *tire.*

14. The kitchen as a very large *sank*.

15. Carpets are used on the *door.*

Activity 5: Quick Draw - Lemonhead Monster

This activity requires the child to listen attentively. Each child (it is better if you have more than one for this activity) will need a piece of paper and a pencil. You will read out the directions allowing enough time to complete each step before moving on to the next step after completion. Each child will share and discuss their drawing and decide if they all look similar. Then ask them if the directions could have been explained better. Which directions or what part of the directions would they change. (You can easily make up your own drawing and directions). Directions for Lemonhead Monster are on the following page.

Lemonhead Monster

Step 1: In the middle of the page, draw a circle.

Step 2: In the middle of the circle, draw a mid-size circle.

Step 3: In the circle, about ¾ of the way down, draw a crooked line.

Step 4: In the top ¼ of the circle, draw 2 small circles spaced apart.

Step 5: On top of the circle, draw straight lines that touch the circle and go outward.

Step 6: On the right side of the circle, draw a half circle.

Step 7: On the left side of the circle, draw another half square.

Activity 6: Lego Build

This activity requires at least 2 players. Player 1 will use Legos to build an object of their choice. They will keep a record of how many Legos they use to build their object, etc. The second step of this project will be to pick a partner (Player 2) and have the person sit back to back with them. Player 1 will give their partner step by step instructions on how to build an object just like the one that they built. Player 2 continues to follow instructions given by Player 1 until their object is completed. Then it will be the second person's turn to give the instructions on how to build the object. After both objects are built, they are to be compared to see if they are the same or different. They can also discuss how the directions could have been given differently if the objects do not turn out similar to one another.

Additional Benefits: This activity requires general knowledge of right and left, where objects are in space and cooperation.

Auditory Processing: Games

Game 1: Listening Lotto

This game lets your child listen to the words and sounds on a CD and place tokens on the images on their game cards that match what they hear. There are many varieties of this game such as indoor sounds, outdoor sounds and words. This game can also be built by you if you are good at electronics. You could actually go outside or inside and tape the sounds around your house and yard. It can be used at any age, but they must like to play bingo!

Additional Benefits: This activity gives extra practice in following directions.

Resource: Listening Lotto is produced by Fun Express and can be found at WalMart.com, Target.com and Amazon.com.

Game 2: Simon Says

This is an old, but very effective game. The more people involved in the game the better, so include your whole family! Designate one person as Simon and the other participants as players. Simon stands in front of the other players and tells them what they must do. Simon will include the words "Simon Says" when the players must obey the commands. If Simon does not include the words, "Simon Says," then they should not follow the command. For example, if Simon says, "Simon says to play the piano", they must pretend to play the piano. If Simon says, "Jump," they should not move. If they do, they are out of the game (if you choose). The last player standing becomes the new Simon and must give directions to the players. The object of "Simon" is to dupe the players and have them follow your commands when they shouldn't.

Additional Benefits: Simon Says helps children to follow directions, balance, and eye-hand coordination.

Game 3: BINGO

This is an all-time favorite and comes in many categories (spelling, reading, geography etc.). The object is to correctly "hear" the numbers and letters being called out, which helps with auditory processing. Challenge your child by buying different categories of the game and varying how the game is won (straight across, four corners, an "x", etc.)

Additional Benefits: Playing Bingo helps with visual perception, following directions, and eye-hand coordination.

Resource: Bingo is produced by Regal Games and can be found at Amazon.com, Target.com and WalMart.com.

Game 4: Mad Gab

This game can be used by individuals and/or teams. The object is to decipher groups of unrelated words into real phrases before time runs out. You will need to repeat the words aloud a few times.

For example, dew wino hue translates into, Do I know you?

This game will cause lots of laughter especially when playing with friends as you are speaking a strange language and trying to figure out what is really being said.

Additional Benefits: Mad Gab encourages cooperation and improves listening skills.

Resource: Mad Gab is produced by Mattel and can be found at most box stores including WalMart.com, Target.com and Amazon.com.

This page left intentionally blank.

Section 4: Visual Perception and Processing

Visual Perception and Processing

Understood.org describes a Visual Perception and Processing disorder as the inability to relate to information being taken in by the eyes and can cause misinterpretation of their environment. There are eight specific types of visual perception and processing difficulties. I suggest you go to Understood.org to read up on all the different types.

School Examples: In school, there are several areas that can be affected such as trouble copying from a book, knowing how far an object is away from their space, reading maps, judging time, recognizing an object when a part is missing, reversing or misreading letters or numbers and skipping lines when reading.

Personal Example: I am currently working with a young lady who is in the fifth grade and has difficulty with discriminating a 'b' from a 'd'. This greatly impacts her ability to read. When reading, she also skips lines of reading and does not see how the sentences do not relate to each other. I currently use the following activities to help her with this.

I have her scan letters on a page and circle the letters assigned to her. She can be given one or two letters at a time so far. I do not give both 'b' and 'd' at the same time, as she needs to have practice selecting the right letter. When she reads and skips a line, I have her tell me how the meanings of sentences are connected together and whether they make sense or not. Given the time she needs, she is able to explain how they are not connected, and I have her re-read the sentence correctly. We also take time out every tutoring session to play a game such as SET that is helping her with processing speed and her ability to see where cards are in space to each other. It also requires her to recognize shapes and likenesses. We also play a short game of Concentration where she has to remember where objects are located and where they are in space. She is progressing nicely. Keep in touch and I will let you know how she is doing!

EnhancingLearningAbilities.com

Visual Perception and Processing: Activities

Activity 1: Optical Illusions

Optical illusions are pictures where you can see multiple objects or persons in one picture. A good example would be the optical illusion where you see either two faces or two vases. The eye only sees one at a time, and it may take a while for someone to find the other image. You can find optical illusion pictures at <u>brainden.com</u>. This can be fun for the whole family as each person will perceive something different. The face illusions are a good place to start. It will give you some of the most used picture illusions. Have fun with this and include the whole family!

Additional Benefits: Have fun!! Improve Imagination!

Note: I have included two of the optical illusions that I used in my dissertation as I was working on my Doctorate degree. Some of the teachers and parents that were part of my group could not find all the pictures included, and I had to put an overlay over the picture to show them what they were unable to find. This picture has both an old lady and a young woman in it. See if you can find both!

Activity 2: Incomplete Pictures of Objects

In this activity, you give the child incomplete pictures of an object and ask them to name the object. It is often difficult for someone to see the whole picture when only part of the object is visible. It is often difficult for someone who is trying to put together a picture puzzle but is unable to picture all the details as a whole. The example on the next page is an eagle. This picture was found on eyecanlearn.com. You can also find these types of pictures at edhelper.com.

If you make your own pictures, you can begin with presenting an almost complete picture and then slowly taking some of the picture away.

Additional Benefits: This activity will help with memory and imagination.

Activity 3: Wordles

This activity requires looking at a picture and deciding what phrase or meaning to give the picture. It uses various symbols and pictures in them. You can find some Wordles at "Wordles List, University of Rhode Island" or www.playmeo.com on the internet. The following pages contain 42 Wordle images with an answer key at the end. These images have been used over the years to help with critical thinking and the source of these pictures is unknown.

Additional Benefits: This activity really helps the imagination, critical thinking skills and the ability to understand phrases that are used in everyday language.

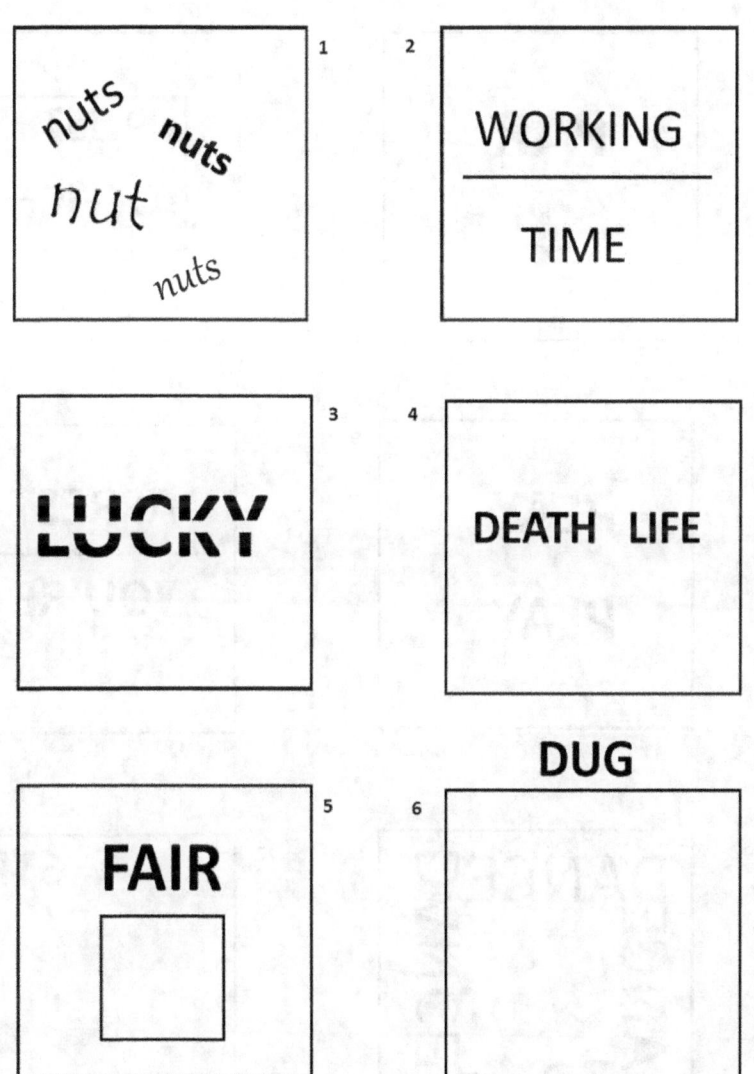

EnhancingLearningAbilities.com

7. PAR / 2

8. POST OFFICE (inside a box)

9. PLAY / PLAY

10. ARREST / YOU'RE

11. DANCE / DANCE / DANCE / DANCE (arranged around the four sides of a square)

12. STR / EET

13. BACK (faded)	14. DECI SION
15. LOVE with HEAD over HEELS	16. I over 8
17. 4 HAND	18. ___ MEN

19

```
e      e     eeeeee    eeeee
e      e        e         e
e      e      eeeee     eeee
e      e        e         e
eeee   e        e       eeeee
```

20

BO PEEP

21

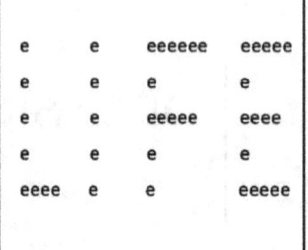

ACE

22

RED

23

MOON
―――――
MIAMI

24

25	26
YEAR YEAR	HEADER HEADER
27	28
DNUORG	TIDE
29	30
STOP	CCCCCCCCCCC

EnhancingLearningAbilities.com

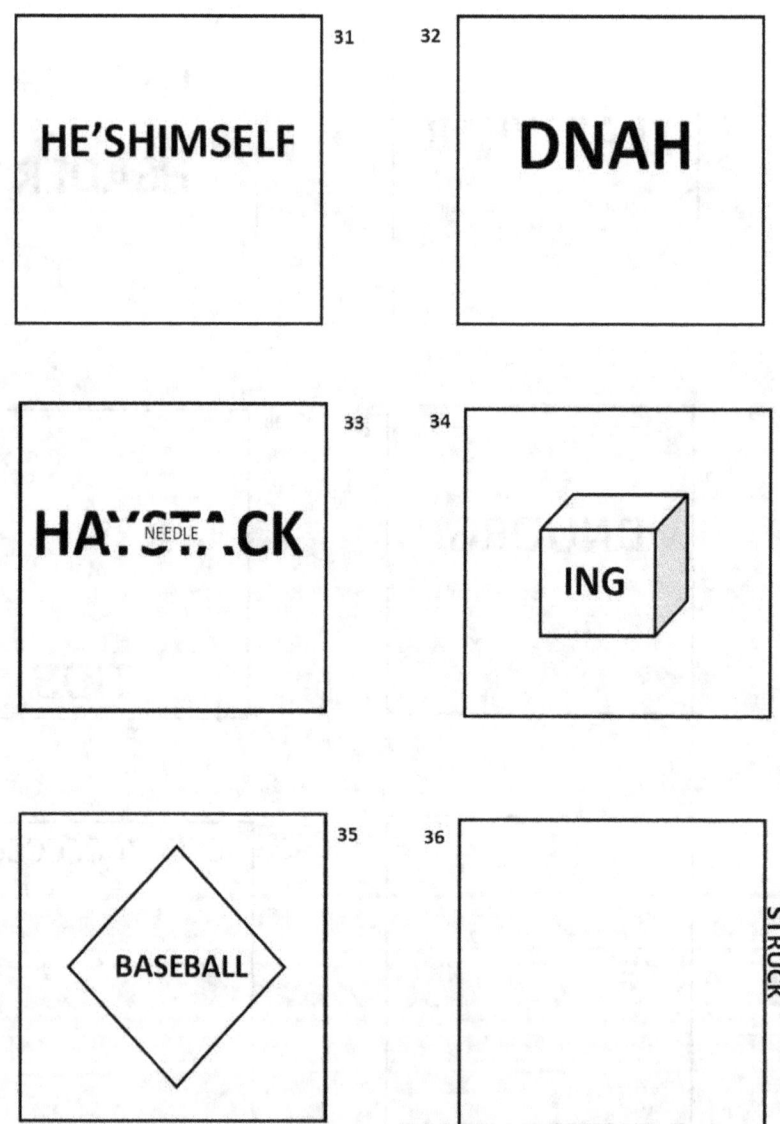

37	38
GETIT	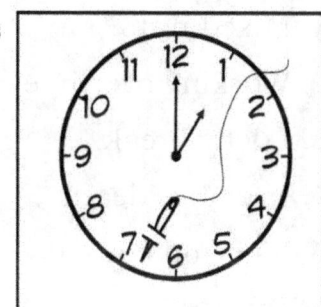

39	40
0 / B.A. / B.S. / P.H.D. / M.A.	SAND

41	42
IN(WAIT)SIDE	BULL / BULL / BULL / BULL I

Wordle Answer Key

1. Mixed nuts
2. Working overtime
3. Lucky break
4. Life after death
5. Fair and square
6. Dug out
7. Two under par
8. Post office box
9. Double play
10. You're under arrest
11. Square dance
12. Street corner
13. Half-back
14. Split decision
15. Head over heels in love
16. I overate
17. Beforehand
18. Linemen
19. Life of ease
20. Little Bo Beep
21. Ace high
22. Big red
23. Moon over Miami
24. Homerun
25. Year after year
26. Double-header
27. Background
28. Low tide
29. Short stop
30. High seas
31. He's beside himself
32. Backhand
33. Needle in a haystack
34. Boxing
35. Baseball diamond
36. Struck out
37. Get with it
38. A stitch in time
39. 4 degrees below zero
40. Sandbox
41. Wait inside
42. Bull's eye

Activity 4: Working with Word Problems

Visualization of a problem or idea allows the child to expand their thinking and come up with different solutions to problems or at least increase the boundaries of the ideas. For example, when your child has math homework with word problems, have them first visualize the problem and at the same time, verbalize the steps they would take to solve the problem. It is necessary for children to be able to "see" the problem like a video. Mel Levine, <u>A Mind at a Time</u>, stated in one of his lectures that being able to "see" the problem is one of the most advantageous benefits in figuring the solution.

Additional Benefits: Word problems can increase critical thinking skills.

Activity 5: Spelling

Spelling is a visual perception activity. A child benefits from having to say, see and feel spelling words. They need to see the parts of a word (chunks, syllables, sound letter association), feel it by writing it out (you can use shaving cream, rice or white sand for them to write in, or use different colors for different parts of words(and say it as they are writing it. Another good way to help students remember how to spell words is to have them physically move. For example, you can have them move around the room as they spell the words out loud, or you can get a small ball and have them throw the ball to you when they say each letter. The act of moving stimulates the body to help with "seeing" the letters.

Additional Benefits: Spelling activities assist with increasing recall.

Activity 6: Trampoline

The use of a trampoline or bouncing mechanism can be used for all types of visual processing and memory activities. For example, when having your child add two numbers, they can jump at each step of the way. For example, [2 (jump)], [+ (jump)], [3 (jump)] is 5 (jump). As they get better at this, you can have them turn one way or another depending if it is an odd or even number. Have them turn right for even numbers, and turn left for odd numbers etc. The trampoline can be used for spelling, remembering facts, etc. Again, movement is the key.

Additional Benefits: Using a trampoline (or bouncing mechanism) can improve balance, memory and coordination.

Visual Perception and Processing: Games

Game 1: SET

This card game was developed by the MENSA Society and gives practice for a variety of skills and requires you to match patterns (shape, number, design and color). The patterns must be either all the same in each of the 3 cards or each card must be different. Example: all 3 cards must be green or 1 card red, 1 card purple and 1 card green. See directions in card set for variations of game. For younger children, use only solid colors in the beginning.

Additional Benefits: SET is one of the most versatile games for children with a learning disability. It helps them be able to scan (which is needed in reading), recognizing patterns and sets (which is important in reading), visual processing (seeing the whole set of cards rather than each individual one separately and visual perception (recognizing the different colors, shapes, fillers and number of objects on a card).

Resource: This game can be found in most bookstores, on-line ordering sites and at setgame.com. The website also includes a free puzzle each day to solve. The puzzle requires you to find six sets of cards. The first three are pretty easy to find, but it gets harder as you find more sets.

Game 2: Monopoly

Directions: Monopoly is a family game and can be paused and come back to it over several days. It is a game that allows you to move around a board, collect money and buy or sell products such as houses, energies, etc. Please follow directions as given in the game. The object of the game is to have the most money at the end. This game includes having to remember what has been bought and sold, problem solving, scanning, using money, collecting money each time you go past "Go". (Heavy on memory processes).

Additional Benefits: Playing Monopoly will increase the ability to use money and being able to plan a strategy to win and increase the ability to scan.

Resource: Monopoly is produced by Hasbro and can be found at <u>Amazon.com</u>, <u>WalMart.com</u> and other box stores.

Game 3: Battleship

This game requires at least 2 players (or you could use teams). Each player places their ships all over the board on their side and the opponent tries to "sink your ships" by calling out coordinates.

You tell the person giving the coordinates whether it was a "hit" or "miss". This allows them to try and find the opponent's ships. The object is to sink all your enemies' ships before they sink your ships. You must keep track of hits and misses until a player sinks all the enemies' ships. The fleet includes a submarine, patrol boat, destroyer, aircraft carrier and battleship.

Additional Benefits: Battleship is a game that will help to improve memory, eye-hand coordination, and critical thinking skills.

Resource: Battleship is produced by Hasbro and can be found at Target.com, WalMart.com and Amazon.com.

Game 4: Connect Four

This well-loved game requires two players in which the players first choose a color and then take turns dropping one colored disc from the top into a seven-column, six row vertically suspended grid. The pieces fall straight down occupying the lowest available space within the column. The object of the game is to be the first to form a horizontal, vertical, or diagonal line of four of one's own discs. It just takes the right moves to win!

Additional Benefits: Connect Four is a good game to increase good sportsmanship, handling frustration, and being a team player.

Resource: Connect Four is produced by Hasbro and can be found at WalMart.com, Target.com and Amazon.com.

Game 5: Slamwich

This game is fast paced and is like Slapjack. It requires at least two players. You must shuffle the cards and make sure they all face in the same direction. Pass out all the cards face down. Make sure all players get the same number of cards. Have each player hold the cards face down. Going in a clockwise direction, one by one each player must flip their top card face up into a pile in the middle. Continue with each player having a turn. You may slap the pile when two cards that are the same are on top of each other. For example, a lettuce card on a lettuce card. (A sandwich is when one card is sandwiched inside two other identical cards. For example, a jelly card, a peanut butter card and a jelly card stacked on each other). The person that slaps the pile first gets all the cards in the pile.

Also, slap the pile when a thief card appears and yell "stop thief" first. Take the pile of cards if you slapped and yelled it first. Look for the muncher card, because when it appears, the next person who would normally put down a card must put down the number of cards the muncher demands. If no sandwich is made, the person who put down the muncher card gets the whole stack of cards.

If there is a sandwich in the muncher, not between a muncher and cards, anyone can slam it and get the cards. You lose if you run out of cards and you win if you have all the cards at the end.

Additional Benefits: This fast-paced game can increase processing speed time, memory and cooperation.

Resource: Slamwich is produced by GameWright and can be found in many stores including <u>Amazon.com</u> and <u>WalMart.com</u>.

Section 5: Logic

Logic

The dictionary describes logic as the system or principles of reasoning applicable to any branch of knowledge or study, or the reason or sound judgment, as in utterances or actions.

The Cambridge English Dictionary describes logic as a particular way of thinking especially one that is reasonable and based on good judgment. For example, the process of coming to the conclusion of who stole a cookie based on who was in the room at the time.

Logic is used in school in literature, sentences, English, Greek, philosophy, science and math. It is used heavily in math and with the new standards used for math; it is imperative that students understand and use logic. It enforces critical thinking, which is used so often in school.

Note: Although Logic is not an underlying issue for the person identified as having a learning disability, it is a major area that is affected and has a great impact on success in the academic environment.

Logic: Activities

Activity 1: Logical Thinking

This activity requires you to read sentences to the participant and ask them to explain what they think happened. Sample questions are located on the following pages, but you are welcome to make up your own. This activity can be played in the car or anywhere you have a few minutes to spare. Make sure you spend time asking why they give the answer they do so they can have practice in explaining their thoughts.

Additional Benefits: This activity also helps increase auditory processing skills, critical thinking skills and imagination.

Logic Questions

Ask your child the following questions:

1. I was blowing up a balloon. There was a loud noise.
   -What do you think happened? (the balloon burst)
2. The tire blew out. The car swerved to the right side of the road.
   -What may happen? (you may have an accident)
3. I forgot about the cake. Smoke poured out of the oven.
   -What happened? (the cake was burned)
4. I fell out of a tree. I could not move my arm.
   -What happened? (I broke my arm)
5. The neighbor's lights were off. The door was lock and the car was not in the garage.
   -What happened? (They went out)
6. The lights went out and the TV stopped working. -What happened? (The electricity went off)
7. The earth trembled and the house shook and the windows rattled.
   -What happened? (earthquake)
8. My shoes were new and the floor had just been waxed. I ran to answer the phone.
   -What could happen? (fall down)
9. The man was very large and the chair was old and weak. He sat down in the chair.
   -What do you think happened? (chair broke)

10. I left some papers on the porch when the sun was shining brightly and it was hot.
    -What do you think happened? (papers warped)
11. The girl screamed and covered her eyes, causing her popcorn to fall on the floor.
    -Where was she? (movies)
12. The green monsters were chasing me. As the alarm clock rang, I opened my eyes and sat up.
    -What had happened? (nightmare)
13. Ellen added 4 cups of detergent to the washing machine.
    -What will happen (will overflow with suds)
14. Mary turned the candle over onto the curtains. They became very hot and smoky.
    -What had happened? (curtains caught on fire)
15. The boy parked the car on a hill and left the brake off.
    -What will happen? (car will roll down the hill)
16. It was freezing outside and white things were falling from the sky.
    -What was happening? (it was snowing)
17. When the family returned home, the front door was wide open and they could not find all their furniture.
    -What had happened? (they had been robbed)
18. The teacher was angry, and the boy was sitting on the seat in the principal's office.
    -What had happened? (boy misbehaved)
19. The children were all dressed in funny costumes and went door to door asking for candy.
    -What was happening? (Halloween)

20. Martha turned on the water in the bathtub and left to get the mail. She stopped to talk to her neighbor for thirty minutes.
    -What happened? (the bathtub overflowed)
21. The man packed his clothes in a hurry and forgot to check his closet for shirts.
    -What happened? (he did not take any shirts on his trip)
22. Jason dropped a penny into the pool.
    -What happened? (it sank)
23. Roger left the freezer door open all day.
    -What happened? (all the food was spoiled/melted)
24. Jerry put some money on the bench in the lunchroom. He went back to get it the next day.
    -What could happen? (money is not there)
25. The bush was dry and brown looking. The little girl forgot to water it for two months.
    -What happened? (it died)

Activity 2: Word Play

This activity allows the child to use critical thinking skills as well as logic. They must be able to give reasons they chose each word. The game can be played with one or more persons. It would be a good family activity to see what each person chooses.

A good way to play this game would be to give each person 20 index cards and have them write down one word on each card. As the first person gives their first word, they can ask if anyone else has the same word. If they do, then all players could say why they chose the word. If no one else has the word, the player moves on to the second word, 3rd word, etc. After the first player goes through his 20 words, the next person talks about the words they chose (not including the ones they agreed with the other player).

Activity: Players will imagine living in a world with only 20 words. What twenty words would they choose and why. Have them write the words on a sheet of paper. Compare differences that each person chose and why.

Additional Benefits: This activity definitely helps with critical thinking as they have to explain why they chose the words they did, patience as each person has to explain their reasoning and good sportsmanship if they disagree.

Activity 3: Survival

This activity has been used in many classrooms, but there is never enough time to really delve into the differences between what the players say. Also, it gives the players a chance to understand what survival really means (Ex: a TV or phone would not be critical on an island with no electricity or phone poles). You read the scenario and have the players name the top 15 items they will need the most, if stranded on an island and had no way of escape. A variation of the game is that they could also have them think of ways they could escape from the island and compare notes from all the players.

The scenario to read to the players is located on the next page.

Additional Benefits: This activity requires critical thinking skills.

Survival Game

You, along with several others, are on a boat that capsized. There are many items floating in the water that you may need on the island you can see from the sea, but each person can only carry 15 items. What 15 items do you choose to take with you? Discuss the varying answers from players.

1.
2.
3.
4.
5.
6.
7.
8.
9.
10.
11.
12.
13.
14.
15.

Activity 4: Free Websites for Logical Thinking

There are numerous free websites available for logical thinking. Below are a few that you might want to check out.

- www.Puzzles.com - riddles
- www.smartestbrain.com - thinking puzzles and mind teasers
- www.puzzlesandriddles.com - lateral thinking
- www.learning-tree.org.uk - matchstick puzzles
- www.iriddler.com - riddles

Check them out for hours of fun!

Logic: Games

Game 1: Backgammon

If you love a challenge, this game is for you and your opponent! It takes a while to grasp all the pieces and parts and the instructions will be located inside the game. This is a complex game, but well worth the effort!

Backgammon is a game for two players, played on a board of twenty-four narrow triangles called points. Backgammon's object is to move all your checkers into your own home board and be the first player to bear off all of your checkers. To start the game, each player throws a single die. This determines who goes first and the numbers to be played. The player throwing the higher number moves first

Additional Benefits: Backgammon provides practice in visual perception, strategy and handling frustration.

Resource: Backgammon is produced by Yenigun and can be found in toy stores as well as box stores such as WalMart.com, Target.com and Amazon.com.

Game 2: Gobblett or Gobblett Junior

This game is like tic-tac-toe but with strategy and memory mixed in. It takes two players and the object is to line up four pieces in a row and win. Begin by stacking all your pieces into 3 piles, by size next to the board. On your turn, take one from the top of any of your piles and place it on a square. If you already have a piece in play, you can use it. Now take turns until someone gets four in a row. But, the pieces you put down are different sizes and can slip over each other. This means the other player can cover your piece and you can cover theirs. So, logically, the bigger your pieces are, the less likely it is that you will get covered. Pieces can also be uncovered, but this can be tricky. Did you leave your opponents pieces under yours? Will picking up your pieces give him an advantage? Try it and see!

Additional Benefits: Gobblett or Gobblett Junior aids in the skill of visual processing and perception, as well as learning the art of strategic thinking.

Resource: Gobblett or Gobblett Jr. is produced by Fun Again and can be found on their website as well as major box stores such as Target.com and WalMart.com.

Game 3: Othello

This game has been going on since the 19th century. It is a two-player game that is quite simple to learn but takes a long time to master! Othello is played on a non-checkered board with 64 discs, which are black on one side and white on the other. One player plays discs black side up and the other player uses white side up. Begin by placing 4 discs in the center of the board, 2 with black side up and 2 with white side up so that the discs with matching colors touch diagonally. You can decide in a variety of ways who goes first, but typically the player with the black disc goes first. The idea of the game is to run out of legal moves. During the game you are trying to surround your opponent's disc with two of your own. You can set a time limit or make moves until no legal moves are left. The player with the most discs wins. More detailed instructions will be included in the game.

Additional Benefits: Playing Othello strengthens the skills of strategy, visual perception, and eye-hand coordination.

Resource: Othello is produced by Cardinal and can be found at Target.com and WalMart.com.

Game 4: Connect Four

This well-loved game requires two players in which the players first choose a color and then take turn dropping one colored disc from the top into a seven-column, six row vertically suspended grid. The pieces fall straight down occupying the lowest available space within the column. The object of the game is to be the first to form a horizontal, vertical, or diagonal line of four of one's own discs. It just takes the right moves to win!

Additional Benefits: Good sportsmanship; handling frustration, team playing.

Resource: Connect Four is produced by Hasbro and can be found at all major stores including WalMart.com, Target.com and Amazon.com.

Game 5: Chocolate Fix

In this game, you are the Baker's Apprentice and you are filling custom candy orders. The problem is all orders have arrived as puzzle clues and you must sort them out using logic to fill the requests and satisfy your customers. To play, pick a challenge and review the clues provided. Using the clues, fill the chocolate tray with all nine chocolate pieces in their correct positions. When you think you have completed an order, flip the page to see the solution.

Additional Benefits: This game provides practice in problem solving and critical thinking.

Resource: Chocolate Fix is produced by Think Fun and can be found at Amazon.com, WalMart.com and Target.com.

This page left intentionally blank.

Section 6: Executive Functioning

Executive Functioning

Executive Functioning skills are the ability to organize cognitive processes. These skills include the ability to plan ahead, prioritize, stop and start accurately, shift between activities and the ability to monitor one's own behavior. There are seven areas of executive functioning which are described below.

1. <u>Goal Setting</u> – Determining the series of tasks you need to complete in order to achieve desired results.

   A. Observable Behaviors
   - Unable to see in the future.
   - Difficulty with setting steps to reach a goal.
   - Doesn't know how to set short-and-long term goals.
   - Works day-to-day without plan.

   B. Intervention Activities
   - Make daily plans and have a checklist to be able to check off each item as it is completed.
   - Begin with setting short term goals, then moving to long term goals.
   - Have them cut out or draw pictures of their goals and put them where they can see them each day.
   - Identify a passion they have and devote time to that passion where they will see and feel success, which may extend to other activities after they see how the work pays off.

- Move from dependence to independence in small steps.
- Talk about the endpoint of a task. (What is it? How do we get there?)
- Use calendars to plan out tasks.

2. <u>Planning and Prioritizing</u> – Improving the ability to set goals and how to reach them; including task initiation.

A. Observable Behaviors
- Inability to complete tasks in a timely manner.
- Inability to decide what information is important and what is not.
- Inability to break down long term assignments.
- Displays procrastination.
- Unable to decide what task needs to get done first.

B. Intervention Activities
- Use a timer so they are aware of time concepts.
- Use a checklist so they can check off each step of a long-term assignment.
- Help with breaking down long-term assignments into manageable chunks along with setting due dates for each step.
- Give them only 1 to 2 minutes before they are required to begin their homework or assigned work on a long-term assignment.
- Prioritize tasks.

3. Organization – Improving the ability to keep track of information both physically and mentally.

Materials Management
A. Observable Behaviors
- Loses items frequently.
- Doesn't remember to bring information home or back to school.
- Doesn't put information in the right place for future use.
- Desk, book bag, books....always a mess!
- Unable to organize books or assignment notebooks.
- Spends long periods of time looking for items he/she needs.

B. Intervention Activities
- Schedule a time to organize book bags, desk, study area, etc each week and always hold that meeting.
- After working on homework/home assignments, make sure they put the information in the correct place.
- Try a few organizational plans and see which one fits for your child - one notebook with dividers or different folders for each academic area, match color of books with color of folders.
- Have a specific area set up for academic pursuits, and have the child clean up the area each time he/she uses it.

Time Management

A. Observable Behaviors
- Loses track of time.
- Cannot estimate how long assignments will take.
- Gets confused with steps or order to complete an assignment.
- Cannot follow multi-step directions.
- Does not understand the importance of time.

B. Intervention Activities
- Keep a record of how long each type of assignment takes.
- Give practice opportunities for time management.
- Develop schedules for daily chores with time limits set.
- Use checklists so they can determine what needs to be done, and don't forget to include time limits.
- Have a set time schedule for completing homework.

Self-Management

A. Observable Behaviors
- Can't change from one activity to another successfully and effectively.
- Trouble with getting started; initiation.
- Slow with routines.
- Trouble with following through on promises or daily responsibilities.

B. Intervention Activities:
- Consistency is key.
- Have set time and space to complete assignment; if no homework, have them work on academics: reading, math, writing.
- Each week, help them organize their spaces (bookbags, desks, notebooks). Full support at first, then progressively have them complete the organization independently.
- Color code folders, books, etc.
- Set timers when working so they can begin to understand time. (Using a timer that shows red for the amount of time allotted is helpful.)
- Talk about how to break down assignments and about how long each part will take.
- Use checklists for daily routines so they can check off what they have completed. (Also good for reminding them so you don't have to nag.)
- Help them prioritize their time and assignments.

4. Remembering – Improving the ability to keep important information in mind (Refer to memory section for more in-depth understanding.)

A. Observable Behaviors
- Cannot complete rote memory activities correctly.
- Fails to write down assignments.
- Fails to turn in completed work.
- Does not remember to do household chores.
- Does not remember homework assignments.

B. Intervention Activities

- Check agendas or calendars daily (move toward independence of these skills slowly).
- Use checklists as reminders; can use electronic devices for reminders.
- Practice memorizing tables, formulas or steps to complete tasks.
- Use cognitive credit cards.

5. Flexible Problem Solving – Improving the ability to adjust to changes.

A. Observable Behaviors
- Doesn't understand what questions are being asked.
- Doesn't understand what the actual problem is in a situation.
- Difficulty with critical thinking skills.
- Difficulty with knowing what skills are needed to solve problem.
- Difficulty with study skills.
- Trouble applying rules.

B. Intervention Activities
- Teach problem solving skills.
- Discuss questions before trying to answer them to determine what is being asked.
- Make connections with what is read and points of view.
- Teach study skills. (There are books that are available.)
- Repeat any rules that are necessary to complete tasks.

6. <u>Self-Monitoring</u> – Improving the ability to evaluate how one is doing on any given situation or task.

A. Observable Behaviors
- Doesn't check over work.
- Doesn't understand social cues.
- Not able to stay on topic.
- Doesn't respond to feedback (or understand it many times).
- Can't see own mistakes.

B. Intervention Activities
- Have child go over the mistakes you find in their work and help them understand where the mistakes are.
- Checklists for staying on task.
- Cognitive credit cards.
- Checklists for turning in assignments.
- Give additional time to complete assignment.

7. <u>Emotional Self-Regulation</u> – Thinking before acting and ability to keep emotions in check.

A. Observable Behaviors
- Doesn't think about consequences before acting.
- Becomes overemotional at simple acts.
- Does not see that they are not able to remain on task due to behavior.
- Causes conflict with no plan of solving the situation.

B. Intervention Activities
- ➤ Teach stop and think method (stop for 5 seconds before acting).
- ➤ Talk to them about their thought patterns when they overreact to simple situations.
- ➤ Video tape them to show them how they act during an assignment (this can be done for homework): as often, they do not see themselves as off task.
- ➤ Teach problem solving techniques

- ➤ Step 1. Identify the problem.
- ➤ Step 2: Brainstorm possible solutions.
- ➤ Step 3: Pick a solution to try.
- ➤ Step 4: Try the solution.
- ➤ Step 5: Review the solution you tried to see if it worked; if it did not, try another one!

The following games and activities will help with one or more of these key functions.

Executive Functioning: Activities & Games

Cursive Handwriting

This activity is vital to helping with executive functioning skills such as planning. This is an important skill that used to be taught in schools; however, there are a lot of students who were not given this instruction and the deficit area of executive functioning skills has increased. You can still buy lined writing paper that is designed to help students visualize the size and practice writing small and capital letters. This activity will require time given to it each day until the child is able to write in cursive on their own. Begin with writing the letters separately in cursive and then teach them how to connect the letters.

Monopoly Board Game

Monopoly is a family game and can be paused and come back to it over several days. It is a game that allows you to move around a board, collect money and buy or sell products such as houses, energies, etc. Please follow directions as given in game. The object of the game is to have the most money at the end. This game includes having to remember what has been bought and sold, problem solving, scanning, using money, collecting money each time you go past "Go". (Heavy on memory processes).

Additional Benefits: Playing Monopoly will increase the ability to use money and being able to plan a strategy to win and increase the ability to scan.

Resource: Monopoly is produced by Hasbro and can be found at Amazon.com, WalMart.com and other box stores.

Sorry Board Game

This game is another strategy game where you will use critical thinking skills as well as visualization. The object of the game is to get all of your pieces to the home spot before any other player does. You can have all of your pieces on the board at the same time. It has some specific rules where you can only leave home with a "2" and you must get exactly the number of spaces you need to go to the finish lines.

Additional Benefits: Playing this game requires a great number of skills that you use in everyday life: strategy, critical thinking, space orientation and visualizing.

Resource: Sorry is available at WalMart.com, Target.com, and Amazon.com.

Glossary

Acronyms - an abbreviation formed from the initial letters of other words and pronounced as a word (Ex: ATM for automated teller machine).

Anagrams - a word, phrase or name formed by rearranging the letters of another (Ex: cinema formed from iceman)

Diagrams - a simplified drawing showing the appearance, structure or workings of something

Elaboration - the addition of more details to information already known

Open-Ended Questions - Questions that require more than a yes or no answer

Paraphrasing - expressing the meaning of something written or spoke using different words, especially to obtain greater clarity

Paired Association - the learning of syllables, digits or words in pairs so that one member of the pair evokes recall of the other word

Rhymes - words have or end with the same sound that corresponds with another word

Sub-vocalization - silent speaking

Summarization - summing up the main points of written or oral information that has been given

This page left intentionally blank.

Resources

Outside Programs

Academic:

The information given below comes directly from the various progams' websites.

PACE - Process and Cognitive Enhancement

PACE is a method of improving one's ability to process and use sensory information to function well in everyday life. It is scientifically based and asserts that training procedures can change and improve the mind and its mental structure by retraining mental skills and processes.

These skills are retrained through a series of tasks that are designed to meet specific goals. The tasks are related, make repetitive demands on a deficient skill, and progressively increase in difficulty. This is a *process-specific approach* to training (as opposed to a general stimulation approach). It also contains a reading component. You can access their website at pacelearningskills.com.

FastForword

Fast ForWord® is a computer-based reading program intended to help students develop and strengthen the cognitive skills necessary for successful reading and learning. The program, which is designed to be used 30 to 100 minutes a day, five days a week, for 4 to 16 weeks, includes two components. More information can be found at What Works Clearinghouse or FastForwordhome.com. Pepin Academies used this program for a while and when used appropriately can show gains in children's reading and learning.

PhonoGraphix Reading Program

The Phono-Graphix Reading Method is a phonetic-linguistic approach to teaching reading, based upon extensive clinical experience with children and rigorous research in the fields of reading, cognitive psychology, learning theory, child development, motivation theory and linguistics.

Phono-Graphix is remarkably straightforward and sensible, encouraging its popularity among teachers and parents since 1993. It has been successfully used in classrooms, clinics, pull-out and RTI programs, bilingual and ESL programs, Waldorf and Montessori schools, pre-schools, home-schools, speech and language pathology practices, volunteer literacy projects and adult literacy programs.

More information can be found on this program at phono-graphix.com.

Outside Programs - Self Regulation

How Does Your Engine Run?

The Alert Program® has boiled down complex theory to create simple, practical solutions you can incorporate into your every day living.

One of the analogies we use with children is, "If your body is like a car engine, sometimes it runs on high (hyped up), sometimes it runs on low (lethargic), and sometimes it runs just right (alert and focused)." But it's not just children. We are all self-regulators.

Think about the ways you self-regulate. Do you need coffee in the morning to wake up? Do you take a brisk walk at lunch to keep you thinking clearly? Do you read before you go to bed to wind down for sleep?

The more we all learn about self-regulation, the better we can handle life's challenges. It helps us bring out our best selves.

You can find more information at AlertProgram.com.

Why Try?

Teach social and emotional principles to youth in a way they can understand and remember. WhyTry is based on sound empirical principles, including solution-focused brief therapy, social and emotional intelligence, and multisensory learning.

The WhyTry curriculum utilizes a series of ten visual analogies that teach important life skills (e.g., decisions have consequences; dealing with with peer pressure; obeying laws and rules; plugging in to support systems).

The visual analogies are reinforced through the creative use of customized hip-hop music, video, over 150 learning activities, journal activities that help students reflect on program concepts, and other multimedia. The WhyTry curriculum engages all major learning styles (visual, auditory, and body-kinesthetic). WhyTry is often used for RTI (Response to Intervention) and PBiS (Positive Behavior intervention Support.)

The WhyTry Program is currently being used in over 20,000 organizations in all 50 of the United States, as well as Canada, the United Kingdom, and Australia.

Please visit their website, whytry.org for more information.

ENHANCING LEARNING ABILITIES

Increase Your Child's Possibilities at the Kitchen Table

"Dr. Scott is a servant leader who puts students first. She uses emerging educational strategies to teach literacy skills that are differentiated for each student. Dr. Scott has led schools that focus on teaching outside of the box to create a school culture that ensures every student is successful both academically and socially."

Dr. Marcos Rodriguez
Assistant Principal
Bloomingdale High School

"Research has shown that our brains are literally 'wired for pleasure'. It is my experience that games are an effective and motivational way to build real world skills. I see students every day improve through game play in problem solving with strategic thinking, memory, collaboration, role playing, exploration and discovery, planning hand-eye coordination, following directions and rules. In addition, there are numerous social interaction benefits. Many of these skills transfer to real world skill application helping to help rewire the brain through motivated play. What better way to build on a deficit area than with motivation and enjoyment."

Denise Morelli
Skills Lab Instructor
Pepin Academies, Riverview

www.ingramcontent.com/pod-product-compliance
Lightning Source LLC
Chambersburg PA
CBHW070109080526
44586CB00013B/1237